FLUTE

101 BROADWAY SONGS

Available for
FLUTE, CLARINET, ALTO SAX, TENOR SAX, TRUMPET,
HORN, TROMBONE, VIOLIN, VIOLA, CELLO

ISBN 978-1-4950-5246-0

7777 W. BLUEMOUND RD. P.O. BOX 13819 MILWAUKEE, WI 53213

Visit Hal Leonard Online at
www.halleonard.com

CONTENTS

ALL I ASK OF YOU

from THE PHANTOM OF THE OPERA

FLUTE

Music by ANDREW LLOYD WEBBER
Lyrics by CHARLES HART
Additional Lyrics by RICHARD STILGOE

ANY DREAM WILL DO

from JOSEPH AND THE AMAZING TECHNICOLOR® DREAMCOAT

Flute

Music by ANDREW LLOYD WEBBER
Lyrics by TIM RICE

ANYTHING YOU CAN DO

from the Stage Production ANNIE GET YOUR GUN

FLUTE

Words and Music by
IRVING BERLIN

AS IF WE NEVER SAID GOODBYE

from SUNSET BOULEVARD

Flute

Music by ANDREW LLOYD WEBBER
Lyrics by DON BLACK and CHRISTOPHER HAMPTON,
with contributions by AMY POWERS

AS LONG AS HE NEEDS ME

from the Broadway Musical OLIVER!

Flute

Words and Music by
LIONEL BART

BALI HA'I
from SOUTH PACIFIC

Flute

Lyrics by OSCAR HAMMERSTEIN II
Music by RICHARD RODGERS

BAUBLES, BANGLES AND BEADS

from KISMET

Flute

Words and Music by ROBERT WRIGHT
and GEORGE FORREST
(Music Based on Themes of A. BORODIN)

Moderately

BROTHERHOOD OF MAN

from HOW TO SUCCEED IN BUSINESS WITHOUT REALLY TRYING

Flute

By FRANK LOESSER

CABARET
from the Musical CABARET

FLUTE

Words by FRED EBB
Music by JOHN KANDER

CAN'T TAKE MY EYES OFF OF YOU

featured in *JERSEY BOYS*

Flute

Words and Music by BOB CREWE
and BOB GAUDIO

CIRCLE OF LIFE

Disney Presents THE LION KING: THE BROADWAY MUSICAL

FLUTE

Music by ELTON JOHN
Lyrics by TIM RICE

Moderately, with an African beat

CLIMB EV'RY MOUNTAIN

from THE SOUND OF MUSIC

Flute

Lyrics by OSCAR HAMMERSTEIN II
Music by RICHARD RODGERS

CLOSE EVERY DOOR

from JOSEPH AND THE AMAZING TECHNICOLOR® DREAMCOAT

Flute

Music by ANDREW LLOYD WEBBER
Lyrics by TIM RICE

DANCING QUEEN

from MAMMA MIA!

Flute

Words and Music by BENNY ANDERSSON,
BJÖRN ULVAEUS and STIG ANDERSON

DEFYING GRAVITY
from the Broadway Musical WICKED

FLUTE

Music and Lyrics by
STEPHEN SCHWARTZ

Tempo I

DO-RE-MI
from THE SOUND OF MUSIC

Flute

Lyrics by OSCAR HAMMERSTEIN II
Music by RICHARD RODGERS

DO YOU HEAR THE PEOPLE SING?

from LES MISÉRABLES

Flute

Music by CLAUDE-MICHEL SCHÖNBERG
Lyrics by ALAIN BOUBLIL, JEAN-MARC NATEL
and HERBERT KRETZMER

March tempo

DON'T CRY FOR ME ARGENTINA

from EVITA

Flute

Words by TIM RICE
Music by ANDREW LLOYD WEBBER

EASTER PARADE
from AS THOUSANDS CHEER

FLUTE

Words and Music by
IRVING BERLIN

EDELWEISS
from THE SOUND OF MUSIC

Flute

Lyrics by OSCAR HAMMERSTEIN II
Music by RICHARD RODGERS

EVERYTHING'S ALRIGHT

from JESUS CHRIST SUPERSTAR

Flute

Words by TIM RICE
Music by ANDREW LLOYD WEBBER

A FOGGY DAY (IN LONDON TOWN)

from A DAMSEL IN DISTRESS

Flute

Music and Lyrics by GEORGE GERSHWIN
and IRA GERSHWIN

GETTING TO KNOW YOU

from THE KING AND I

Flute

Lyrics by OSCAR HAMMERSTEIN II
Music by RICHARD RODGERS

FRIEND LIKE ME

(Stageplay Version)

from the Walt Disney Stageplay ALADDIN

Flute

Music by ALAN MENKEN
Lyrics by HOWARD ASHMAN
and STEPHEN SCHWARTZ

GUYS AND DOLLS

from GUYS AND DOLLS

Flute

By FRANK LOESSER

HELLO, DOLLY!

from HELLO, DOLLY!

Flute

Music and Lyric by
JERRY HERMAN

HOME

from Walt Disney's BEAUTY AND THE BEAST: THE BROADWAY MUSICAL

Flute

Music by ALAN MENKEN
Lyrics by TIM RICE

Moderately

HOW ARE THINGS IN GLOCCA MORRA
from FINIAN'S RAINBOW

Flute

Words by E.Y. "YIP" HARBURG
Music by BURTON LANE

I BELIEVE IN YOU
from HOW TO SUCCEED IN BUSINESS WITHOUT REALLY TRYING

Flute

By FRANK LOESSER

I DON'T KNOW HOW TO LOVE HIM

from JESUS CHRIST SUPERSTAR

Flute

Words by TIM RICE
Music by ANDREW LLOYD WEBBER

I DREAMED A DREAM

from LES MISÉRABLES

Flute

Music by CLAUDE-MICHEL SCHÖNBERG
Lyrics by ALAIN BOUBLIL, JEAN-MARC NATEL
and HERBERT KRETZMER

I GOT PLENTY O' NUTTIN'

from PORGY AND BESS®

Flute

Music and Lyrics by GEORGE GERSHWIN,
DuBOSE and DORTHY HEYWARD
and IRA GERSHWIN

I WHISTLE A HAPPY TUNE

from THE KING AND I

Flute

Lyrics by OSCAR HAMMERSTEIN II
Music by RICHARD RODGERS

I'VE NEVER BEEN IN LOVE BEFORE

from GUYS AND DOLLS

Flute

By FRANK LOESSER

IF I LOVED YOU

from CAROUSEL

Flute

Lyrics by OSCAR HAMMERSTEIN II
Music by RICHARD RODGERS

Slowly

IF I WERE A BELL

from GUYS AND DOLLS

FLUTE

By FRANK LOESSER

IF I WERE A RICH MAN

from the Musical FIDDLER ON THE ROOF

Flute

Words by SHELDON HARNICK
Music by JERRY BOCK

THE IMPOSSIBLE DREAM

(The Quest)

from MAN OF LA MANCHA

Lyric by JOE DARION
Music by MITCH LEIGH

Flute

IT AIN'T NECESSARILY SO

from PORGY AND BESS®

Flute

Music and Lyrics by GEORGE GERSHWIN,
DuBOSE and DOROTHY HEYWARD
and IRA GERSHWIN

THE LADY IS A TRAMP
from BABES IN ARMS

FLUTE

Words by LORENZ HART
Music by RICHARD RODGERS

THE LAST NIGHT OF THE WORLD

from MISS SAIGON

Flute

Music by CLAUDE-MICHEL SCHÖNBERG
Lyrics by ALAIN BOUBLIL and RICHARD MALTBY JR.
Adapted from original French Lyrics by ALAIN BOUBLIL

LET'S CALL THE WHOLE THING OFF

from SHALL WE DANCE

Flute

Music and Lyrics by GEORGE GERSHWIN
and IRA GERSHWIN

LOVE IS HERE TO STAY

from GOLDWYN FOLLIES

Flute

Music and Lyrics by GEORGE GERSHWIN
and IRA GERSHWIN

LOVE ME OR LEAVE ME
from WHOOPEE!

Flute

Lyrics by GUS KAHN
Music by WALTER DONALDSON

LOVE WALKED IN

from GOLDWYN FOLLIES

Flute

Music and Lyrics by GEORGE GERSHWIN
and IRA GERSHWIN

LUCK BE A LADY
from GUYS AND DOLLS

Flute

By FRANK LOESSER

MAKIN' WHOOPEE!

from WHOOPEE!

Flute

Lyrics by GUS KAHN
Music by WALTER DONALDSON

MAME

from MAME

FLUTE

Music and Lyric by
JERRY HERMAN

MAMMA MIA
from MAMMA MIA!

Flute

Words and Music by BENNY ANDERSSON,
BJÖRN ULVAEUS and STIG ANDERSON

MATCHMAKER
from the Musical FIDDLER ON THE ROOF

Flute

Words by SHELDON HARNICK
Music by JERRY BOCK

MAYBE
from the Musical Production ANNIE

Flute

Lyric by MARTIN CHARNIN
Music by CHARLES STROUSE

MEMORY

from CATS

Flute

Music by ANDREW LLOYD WEBBER
Text by TREVOR NUNN after T.S. ELIOT

THE MUSIC OF THE NIGHT
from THE PHANTOM OF THE OPERA

Flute

Music by ANDREW LLOYD WEBBER
Lyrics by CHARLES HART
Additional Lyrics by RICHARD STILGOE

Moderately slow

MY FAVORITE THINGS

from THE SOUND OF MUSIC

Flute

Lyrics by OSCAR HAMMERSTEIN II
Music by RICHARD RODGERS

NICE WORK IF YOU CAN GET IT

from A DAMSEL IN DISTRESS

Flute

Music and Lyrics by GEORGE GERSHWIN
and IRA GERSWIN

OH, WHAT A BEAUTIFUL MORNIN'

from OKLAHOMA!

FLUTE

Lyrics by OSCAR HAMMERSTEIN II
Music by RICHARD RODGERS

OKLAHOMA
from OKLAHOMA!

Lyrics by OSCAR HAMMERSTEIN II
Music by RICHARD RODGERS

Flute

OL' MAN RIVER
from SHOW BOAT

Flute

Lyrics by OSCAR HAMMERSTEIN II
Music by JEROME KERN

OLD DEVIL MOON

from FINIAN'S RAINBOW

Flute

Words by E.Y. "YIP" HARBURG
Music by BURTON LANE

ON MY OWN

from LES MISÉRABLES

Flute

Music by CLAUDE-MICHEL SCHÖNBERG
Lyrics by ALAIN BOUBLIL, JEAN-MARC NATEL,
HERBERT KRETZMER, JOHN CAIRD
and TREVOR NUNN

Moderately slow

ONCE IN A LIFETIME

from the Musical Production STOP THE WORLD—I WANT TO GET OFF

Flute

Words and Music by LESLIE BRICUSSE
and ANTHONY NEWLEY

ONCE IN LOVE WITH AMY

from WHERE'S CHARLEY?

Flute

By FRANK LOESSER

ONE
from A CHORUS LINE

Music by MARVIN HAMLISCH
Lyric by EDWARD KLEBAN

Flute

PEOPLE WILL SAY WE'RE IN LOVE
from OKLAHOMA!

Lyrics by OSCAR HAMMERSTEIN II
Music by RICHARD RODGERS

Flute

THE PHANTOM OF THE OPERA
from THE PHANTOM OF THE OPERA

Flute

Music by ANDREW LLOYD WEBBER
Lyrics by CHARLES HART
Additional Lyrics by RICHARD STILGOE
and MIKE BATT

Moderately fast

POPULAR
from the Broadway Musical WICKED

FLUTE

Music and Lyrics by
STEPHEN SCHWARTZ

SEASONS OF LOVE

from RENT

Flute

Words and Music by
JONATHAN LARSON

SEND IN THE CLOWNS
from the Musical A LITTLE NIGHT MUSIC

Flute

Words and Music by
STEPHEN SONDHEIM

SEVENTY SIX TROMBONES

from Meredith Willson's THE MUSIC MAN

FLUTE

By MEREDITH WILLSON

SHALL WE DANCE?

from THE KING AND I

Flute

Lyrics by OSCAR HAMMERSTEIN II
Music by RICHARD RODGERS

Lively

SHE LOVES ME

from SHE LOVES ME

Flute

Words by SHELDON HARNICK
Music by JERRY BOCK

Moderately bright

SHERRY
featured in JERSEY BOYS

FLUTE

Words and Music by
BOB GAUDIO

SOME ENCHANTED EVENING

from SOUTH PACIFIC

Flute

Lyrics by OSCAR HAMMERSTEIN II
Music by RICHARD RODGERS

SUMMERTIME

from PORGY AND BESS®

Flute

Music and Lyrics by GEORGE GERSHWIN,
DuBOSE and DOROTHY HEYWARD
and IRA GERSHWIN

SUNRISE, SUNSET

from the Musical FIDDLER ON THE ROOF

Flute

Words by SHELDON HARNICK
Music by JERRY BOCK

SUPERSTAR
from JESUS CHRIST SUPERSTAR

FLUTE

Words by TIM RICE
Music by ANDREW LLOYD WEBBER

THE SURREY WITH THE FRINGE ON TOP

from OKLAHOMA!

Flute

Lyrics by OSCAR HAMMERSTEIN II
Music by RICHARD RODGERS

THE SWEETEST SOUNDS

from NO STRINGS

Flute

Lyrics and Music by
RICHARD RODGERS

THERE'S NO BUSINESS LIKE SHOW BUSINESS

from the Stage Production ANNIE GET YOUR GUN

FLUTE

Words and Music by
IRVING BERLIN

THEY ALL LAUGHED

from SHALL WE DANCE

Flute

Music and Lyrics by GEORGE GERSHWIN
and IRA GERSHWIN

THEY CAN'T TAKE THAT AWAY FROM ME

from SHALL WE DANCE

Flute

Music and Lyrics by GEORGE GERSHWIN
and IRA GERSHWIN

THINK OF ME
from THE PHANTOM OF THE OPERA

FLUTE

Music by ANDREW LLOYD WEBBER
Lyrics by CHARLES HART
Additional Lyrics by RICHARD STILGOE

THIS IS THE MOMENT
from JEKYLL & HYDE

Flute

Words and Music by LESLIE BRICUSSE
and FRANK WILDHORN

THIS NEARLY WAS MINE

from SOUTH PACIFIC

Flute

Lyrics by OSCAR HAMMERSTEIN II
Music by RICHARD RODGERS

TILL THERE WAS YOU

from Meredith Willson's THE MUSIC MAN

Flute

By MEREDITH WILLSON

Moderately

TOMORROW

from the Musical Production ANNIE

Flute

Lyric by MARTIN CHARNIN
Music by CHARLES STROUSE

Moderately slow

WALK LIKE A MAN

featured in JERSEY BOYS

Flute

Words and Music by BOB CREWE
and BOB GAUDIO

UNUSUAL WAY

from NINE

FLUTE

Music and Lyrics by
MAURY YESTON

WHAT I DID FOR LOVE

from A CHORUS LINE

Flute

Music by MARVIN HAMLISCH
Lyric by EDWARD KLEBAN

WHAT KIND OF FOOL AM I?

from the Musical Production STOP THE WORLD—I WANT TO GET OFF

Flute

Words and Music by LESLIE BRICUSSE
and ANTHONY NEWLEY

WHERE IS LOVE?

from the Broadway Musical OLIVER!

Flute

Words and Music by
LIONEL BART

WHO CAN I TURN TO
(When Nobody Needs Me)

from THE ROAR OF THE GREASEPAINT—THE SMELL OF THE CROWD

Flute

Words and Music by LESLIE BRICUSSE
and ANTHONY NEWLEY

A WHOLE NEW WORLD
from the Walt Disney Stageplay ALADDIN

Flute

Music by ALAN MENKEN
Lyrics by TIM RICE

WILL YOU LOVE ME TOMORROW
(Will You Still Love Me Tomorrow)
from BEAUTIFUL

Words and Music by GERRY GOFFIN
and CAROLE KING

Flute

WITH ONE LOOK
from SUNSET BOULEVARD

Flute

Music by ANDREW LLOYD WEBBER
Lyrics by DON BLACK and CHRISTOPHER HAMPTON,
with contributions by AMY POWERS

Moderately slow

WRITTEN IN THE STARS

from Elton John and Tim Rice's AIDA

Flute

Music by ELTON JOHN
Lyrics by TIM RICE

YOU RULE MY WORLD

from THE FULL MONTY

FLUTE

Words and Music by
DAVID YAZBEK

YOU'LL NEVER WALK ALONE

from CAROUSEL

Flute

Lyrics by OSCAR HAMMERSTEIN II
Music by RICHARD RODGERS

YOU'LL BE IN MY HEART

Disney Presents TARZAN The Broadway Musical

FLUTE

Words and Music by
PHIL COLLINS

YOU'VE GOT A FRIEND

from BEAUTIFUL

FLUTE

Words and Music by
CAROLE KING

Fine

D.S. al Fine
(take 1st ending)

YOUNGER THAN SPRINGTIME
from SOUTH PACIFIC

FLUTE

Lyrics by OSCAR HAMMERSTEIN II
Music by RICHARD RODGERS